MY NATURE JOURNAL

A Personal
Nature Guide for Young People

Written and
Illustrated by

ADRIENNE OLMSTEAD

This Book Belongs To

Alana Sunseri

For information about permission to reproduce selections from this book, write to
My Nature Journal Permissions
Pajaro
3343 Las Huertas Rd., Lafayette, CA 94549

Publisher's Cataloging-in-Publication Data (Provided by Quality Books, Inc.)

Olmstead, Adrienne
    My nature journal : a personal nature guide for young people /
    written and illustrated by Adrienne Olmstead. -- 1st ed.
    Includes index.
    ISBN: 0-9672459-1-5
    SUMMARY: Nature activities including leaf rubbings, scavenger hunts,
    magnifying glass examinations, sketching and charting, to be done in
    meadows and woodlands, or at ponds, streams and seashores, by daylight
    or twilight.

        1. Nature study--Activity programs--Juvenile
    literature. 2. Nature history--Outdoor books--
    Juvenile literature   I. Title

QH48.O55 1999   508
                          QBI99-1031

First edition © 2000
10 9 8 7 6 5 4 3 2
Printed in China

CONTENTS

A NOTE TO PARENTS AND EDUCATORS

Helping A Child Build A Personal Connection With Nature

MY NATURE JOURNAL was specifically created as a guide to help children build a strong and lasting personal connection with nature. This journal is designed for children ages 8 and up. It offers three types of activities that enable children to feel closer to nature:

- *DISCOVERY activities* encourage children to explore the natural world: the insects living under leaves on the forest floor, shells on a beach, tadpoles in a pond. Each new discovery sparks children's curiosity about nature. *Woodland Scavenger Hunt* (p. 20) and *Bird-watching Bingo* (p. 102) are two examples of discovery activities.

- *UNDERSTANDING NATURE activities* help children learn basic ecological principles. Where does dirt come from? Why can birds fly? How do bats hunt insects in the dark? Children develop an understanding that everything in nature is important as they learn how nature works. *Spiders Are Spinners* (p. 68) and *My Moon Phase Chart* (p. 152) are two examples of under-standing nature activities.

- *REFLECTIVE activities* inspire children to express their feelings about themselves and nature. Children write how they feel when they spend time alone in nature or they describe their special place in a woodland. Children deepen their connection to nature as they write about their thoughts and experiences. *Magical Meadow* (p. 73) and *Sunset Sit* (p. 136) are two examples of reflective activities.

Why A Journal?

Journals are special in many ways. Nature writing and journal sketching help children increase their awareness of the natural world around them. Children slow down, focus and use their observation skills to capture their nature experiences in their journals.

Journals are also personal books, where children write their thoughts, feelings and discoveries. Children treasure their journals because they are their own creations.

Adult Support

A child's experiences and feelings can be strengthened if they are shared with another person . . .

PARENTS: You can foster your child's relationship with nature by keeping a nature journal yourself and doing the activities alongside your child. Your presence and participation will inspire your child to share his or her discoveries and feelings with you.

EDUCATORS: You can be role models to your students by showing them how to explore the natural world. Woodlands, meadows, streams and seashores are all classrooms. You can use MY NATURE JOURNAL to support your students in their own discovery, learning and appreciation of nature.

IMPORTANT NOTE

Adult supervision is recommended for all activities in this book. The publisher and author assume no responsibility for damages or injuries which may be incurred while performing any of the activities in this book, some of which could be dangerous in certain situations.

"That's for me!"

YOU are about to embark on an **ADVENTURE** into nature. Your adventure is going to be filled with exploration, discovery, learning and surprises. Before you begin your journey through the five natural worlds of this book, be sure you are well equipped. Take good walking shoes, comfortable clothing, a small pack with food and water, drawing tools and your guide along the journey ... MY NATURE JOURNAL.

HOW TO USE YOUR NATURE JOURNAL

There are five sections in your journal: WOODLANDS, MEADOWS, PONDS & STREAMS, SEASHORE and TWILIGHT. You can start your journey in any section and skip from one page to another. The blank pages at the end of each section are for your sketches and your writings, or you can use them to create your own activities.

In each section you can **STUDY** the pages that **EXPLAIN** an aspect of nature, such as

- *Why do plants have leaves?*
- *What lives in tidepools?*
- *What are pollinators?*

These pages help you understand how nature works. Explanations of **underlined** words are in the GLOSSARY at the back of the book.

You can also **DO** the **ACTIVITY** pages where you get to:

- *Explore, listen and search for nature's wonders.*
- *Sketch and describe what you discover.*
- *Write your thoughts and feelings.*

*. . . Remember to fill in the **date** and the **place** (where you are) at the top of the activity pages.*

It is best to do the activities when you are outside and in the right environment. For example, you should be in a woodland when you do the *Woodland Scavenger Hunt* and at the seashore when you do the *Seashore Treasure Trove*.

You can do these activities on your own or with another person. Ask an adult for help if there is a page in your journal that you don't understand.

Look for MY NATURE WRITINGS pages throughout the book. These are special pages where you can **EXPRESS** your **THOUGHTS** and **FEELINGS** about nature.

I Did It ✓

Use MY NATURE LIST at the back of the book to keep a list of animals and plants you **FIND.**

FIVE NATURAL WORLDS
TOPICS & ACTIVITIES

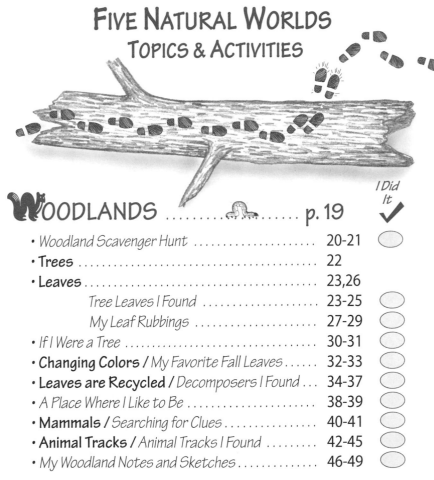

WOODLANDS . . . . **p. 19**

I Did It ✓

MEADOWS .... p. 51

PONDS & STREAMS ......p. 83

$\mathbb{S}$EASHORE .... p. 115

$\mathbb{T}$WILIGHT .... p. 135

BEING SAFE...

As you explore nature, it is important that you stay safe. Exploring nature is fun, but not if you get hurt. These rules will help you be safe while you explore nature.

1. Always get permission from an adult before you explore -- be sure you tell an adult where you are going.
2. Stay on trails.
3. Never wade or swim in water alone.
4. Know which plants to stay away from and how to identify them -- poison oak, poison ivy, poison sumac, stinging nettle.
5. Do not touch or feed wild animals.
6. Do not eat wild plants, mushrooms or berries.
7. Wear comfortable clothes appropriate for the weather and sturdy shoes. Wear a hat and use sunscreen.
8. Carry water to drink when you hike. Don't drink from streams, rivers or lakes.

"Good ru

Can you think of **OTHER WAYS** to be safe when you're in nature?

9. _____

10. _____

11. _____

12. _____

13. _____

. . . AND RESPECTFUL OF NATURE

What does it mean to be respectful? One way you can be respectful is to treat nature the way you like to be treated. These guidelines will help you be respectful of nature:

1. Keep distance between yourself and wild animals. If you stay away and remain quiet, wild animals may remain where you can watch them instead of running away.
2. Be gentle with small creatures, such as insects.
3. Do not pick plants or wildflowers.
4. Keep nature clean of litter.
5. Leave animals and insects where you find them.

See if you can list **FIVE MORE** ways that you can be respectful of nature.

6. _____

7. _____

8. _____

9. _____

10. _____

FIELD SKETCHING

Every single thing in nature is one of a kind. No two things are exactly alike. Drawing -- or field sketching -- is a good way to see how everything in nature is different . . . and beautiful.

TIPS FOR SKETCHING

1. **Draw things you like.** Draw things you are curious about -- things you want to know more about.

2. **Don't worry about what your drawing looks like!** It is more important to look closely and learn from your drawings than to draw a pretty picture. It's OK if your sketches are rough -- they're supposed to be!

3. **Look closely and notice as many details as you can** when you are sketching in your journal. Pay attention to how each thing is shaped and how it is colored. If you do this, your sketches will show how everything in nature is one of a kind.

4. **Look at what you are drawing** just as much (or more) as you look at your page. You have to look closely at what you are drawing to see details.

5. Animals move, so you have to draw quickly!
When drawing an animal, start with a quick
outline. If the animal is still visible when
you are done, start drawing the details.

6. Be careful where you start drawing on
the page. Will you have enough room, or
will your drawing go off the page?

7. Write notes next to your sketches. You
can write the date, your location, and the
name of what you are drawing (if you know it).
Also write any observations you noticed or
anything you would like
to remember.

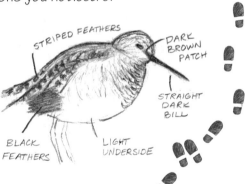

THIS BIRD IS A WILLET.
I SAW IT FEEDING IN
THE SAND AT THE
SEASHORE. WILLETS
HAVE BLACK AND
WHITE FEATHERS
ON THEIR WING
WHICH CAN BE SEEN
WHEN THEY FLY.

STRIPED FEATHERS

DARK
BROWN
PATCH

STRAIGHT
DARK
BILL

BLACK
FEATHERS

LIGHT
UNDERSIDE

It's a good idea to make up a journal kit filled with your
favorite sketching tools. Keep it with your nature journal
so you always have the right tools available. Look on the
next page for suggested items.

MY JOURNAL KIT

The following things are helpful and fun to have in your journal kit when you go exploring in nature:

- **Regular pencils** -- use them for most of your sketching

PENCIL

- **Colored pencils** -- because nature is very colorful!

- A **pencil sharpener**

PENCIL SHARPENER

COLORED PENCILS

- A **good eraser**

ERASER

- A **hand-held magnifier**
-- so you can take a closer look at a tree leaf, or grains of sand, or whatever you like!

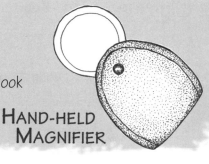

HAND-HELD MAGNIFIER

A **magnifying box** -- so you can look at small creatures more closely. Please remember to always put wildlife back where you found it.

MAGNIFYING
BOX

A **measuring tape** -- use it to measure things you find . . . tracks, wildflowers, shells, anything!

MEASURING TAPE

1

2

3

4

5

6

"I'm ready to go!"

WOODLANDS

WOODLAND SCAVENGER HUNT

Woodlands are natural wonderlands. Many things are hidden just out of sight -- behind logs, under bushes and in the trees. Look closely . . . be a detective. Search high and low. See if you can find everything on the scavenger hunt. Write what you find on the lines. Can you find . . .

*Something **older** than yourself?*

_____

*Something **smaller** than your **thumb**?*

_____

*Something that **flies**?*

_____

*Something **taller** than you?*

_____

*Something that **needs air**?*

_____

*Something **younger** than yourself?*

_____

*Something that **makes you laugh**?*

_____

*Something that is **important**?*

_____

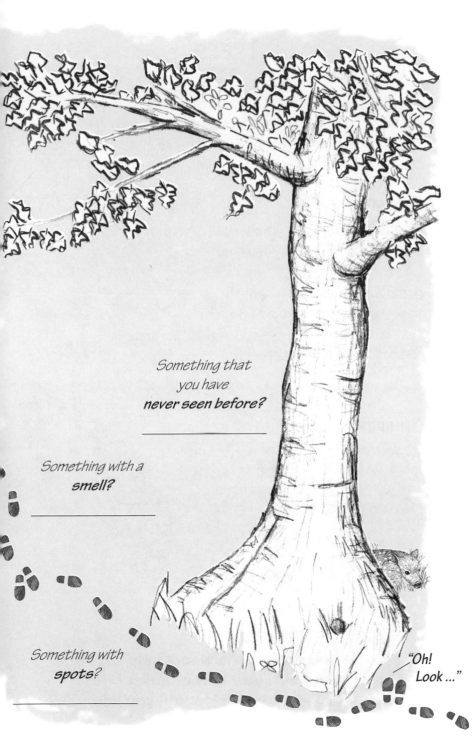

Something that
you have
never seen before?

_____

Something with a
smell?

_____

Something with
spots?

_____

"Oh!
Look ..."

TREES...

Trees are plants with tall, woody trunks. Trees developed their trunks to reach upward toward sunlight and strong roots to stay upright. The two most common groups of trees are **broadleaf** trees and **conifers**.

BROADLEAF

Most broadleaf trees have broad thin leaves. Many kinds lose their leaves in the fall -- these are called **deciduous** trees. All broadleaf trees reproduce by growing flowers that produce seeds. The seeds fall to the ground so that new trees can sprout.

Maple Leaf

A maple tree is an example of a broadleaf tree.

CONIFERS

Conifers have sharp, narrow leaves (often called needles). Most conifers keep their leaves for 3-4 years and so they are called **evergreen**. Instead of growing flowers, these trees have cones that produce seeds.

Douglas Fir cone and needles

A Douglas Fir tree is an example of a conifer.

As you explore the woodlands, examine the trees. Are they broadleaf trees or conifers? How can you tell?

. . . AND THEIR LEAVES

There are many different kinds -- or **species** -- of trees. How can you learn to identify one species of tree from another? One way is to look at the leaves, because each kind of tree has its own kind of leaf.

Explore the woodlands and find as many different kinds of trees as you can.

For each kind of tree you find, collect a leaf and draw or trace its outline on the next two pages in your journal.

Write notes next to your sketches. Is the leaf smooth or fuzzy? Does it have a smell? How long is the leaf? How wide?

If you have a tree identification book, you can use your leaf drawings to look up which tree species you found.

One of the best ways to get to know trees is to get to know their leaves.

TREE LEAVES I FOUND

TREE LEAVES I FOUND

WHY DO PLANTS HAVE LEAVES ...

If you were a hungry plant, you could make your own food.

There are three things you would need:
1) sunlight
2) water
3) carbon dioxide

SUNLIGHT

Plants absorb sunlight through their leaves. Leaves have a green chemical called **chlorophyll** that absorbs sunlight. Chlorophyll changes energy from sunlight into food energy for the plant.

WATER

Plants take up water through their roots. Water travels from the roots to the stem and then upward to the leaves.

CARBON DIOXIDE

Carbon dioxide is a natural gas you create when you breathe. Take a deep breath. You are breathing in **oxygen**. Now, breathe out. You are exhaling carbon dioxide. Plants use the carbon dioxide that you exhale to help make their food.

How do plants make food using sunlight, water and carbon dioxide? Plants use the energy in sunlight to change water and carbon dioxide into sugar. The sugar is food for plants and gives plants energy to grow. If you have ever tasted maple syrup, then you have tasted plant sugar.

The process plants use to make food using sunlight, water and carbon dioxide is called **photosynthesis**.

So, why do plants have leaves? To make their own food!

. . . AND WHY DO THEY DROP THEM?

Many trees get ready for winter by dropping their leaves.

In wintertime, trees can't take in water if the ground is frozen, so trees have to survive on water stored in their trunks and branches. Since leaves use a lot of water, trees drop their leaves in winter. This helps them save water.

Trees also drop their leaves in winter because the days are shorter. Leaves need sunlight to make food, so trees drop their leaves when there is less sunlight.

Some trees, such as conifers, are well adapted to living in cold places and do not need to drop their leaves.

LEAF RUBBINGS

You can make beautiful leaf rubbings in your journal. Gather some leaves that you like from the ground.

Place the leaves under the "My Leaf Rubbings" pages. It works best if you place the leaves with their undersides facing up.

Using crayons, pencils or colored pencils, rub evenly across the page. The image of the leaves underneath will appear.

Try using different colors on the page.

"Cool"

MY LEAF RUBBINGS

MY LEAF RUBBINGS

IF I WERE A TREE

Have you ever wondered how it would feel to be a tree? You would be anchored in the ground your whole life. Birds would nest in your branches. Squirrels would scamper up your trunk. You would eat sunlight, carbon dioxide and water. You would grow tall and bend in the wind.

How would it feel to be a tree?

TREE WRITING

Sit down near a tree that you like. Take a few moments to watch the tree. Imagine the whole life of the tree . . . from a seed in the ground to the tree before you.

How many seasons has it lived through? How many animals have lived in its branches? Imagine that you are that tree.

On the next page, write the life story of the tree as if you were the tree.

Begin as a seed in the ground and continue to today.

MY LIFE AS A TREE

My life began in the ground... _____

_____

_____

_____

_____

_____

_____

_____

_____

_____

_____

_____

_____

_____

_____

_____

_____

_____

_____

_____

_____

_____

_____

_____

_____

_____

_____

_____

_____

_____

_____

WHY DO LEAVES CHANGE COLOR IN FALL?

Leaves are green because they have a green chemical called **chlorophyll**. Leaves also have yellow, red and orange **pigments**, but the green chlorophyll covers up these other colors. In the fall, when trees are dropping their leaves, the green chlorophyll drains away and the yellow and red colors are exposed. This is why leaves change color.

**Explore a woodland in the fall.
Find leaves that are changing color.
Which leaves do you like the best?**

**Draw your favorite fall leaves in your journal.
Why are they your favorite?**

 **MY FAVORITE FALL LEAVES**

MY FAVORITE FALL LEAVES

FALLEN LEAVES ARE RECYCLED

If trees drop their leaves every winter, then why aren't wood-lands buried in ten feet of fallen leaves? Where do the fallen leaves go?

Fallen leaves on the forest floor are called leaf litter. Underneath the top layer of leaf litter, **decomposers** are eating the bottom leaves. What are decomposers? Bacteria, fungus, slugs, insects and other **invertebrates** are all decomposers. Decomposers eat fallen leaves and turn the leaves into soil. The soil helps new plants to grow.

Here's how fallen leaves are recycled:

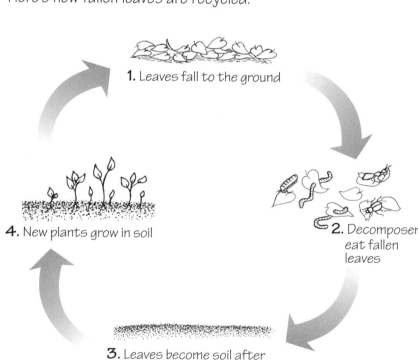

1. Leaves fall to the ground

2. Decomposers eat fallen leaves

3. Leaves become soil after being eaten, digested and **excreted** by decomposers.

4. New plants grow in soil

FINDING DECOMPOSERS

Snail

Beetle

Find out what lives in the leaf litter or soil underneath a tree. Gently pull back the leaf litter and search for decomposers.

You can place a decomposer in a container or magnifying box to get a closer look (remember to put it back where you found it). **You can also use a magnifying glass.**

Ants

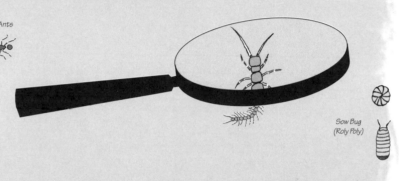

Sow Bug
(Roly Poly)

List or draw the decomposers you find on the next two pages.

•• Thank You For Treating Decomposers With Respect ••

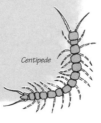
Centipede

Worm

DECOMPOSERS I FOUND

Decomposers I Found

Inch Worm

A Place Where I Like To Be

Spending quiet time in nature is wonderful, especially if you have a special place. A special place is somewhere you like to be. It can be a place that you visit once or many times. Maybe you go to your special place with other people, or maybe you go alone. Your special place may be under a tree or on a rock. It can be anywhere.

Why I Like my Special Place

Find a place in the woodlands that feels special to you . . . a place where you like to be. Describe your special place and why you like it. Drawing a picture of your special place will help you remember it for your whole life.

MY DRAWING OF MY SPECIAL PLACE

WHAT IS A MAMMAL?

What do you have in common with a fox, a raccoon and a squirrel? You are all mammals!

All mammals (including you) are animals that . . .

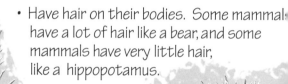
Fox

• Are warm blooded. This means that the temperature inside their bodies stays the same, even when the temperature outside changes.

• Have hair on their bodies. Some mammals have a lot of hair like a bear, and some mammals have very little hair, like a hippopotamus.

• Drink milk from their mothers when they are young.

Raccoon

• Have lungs and breathe air.

• Have bones, including a backbone.

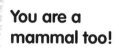
Squirrel

You are a mammal too!

Draw a picture of yourself.

SEARCHING FOR CLUES

It is rare to see mammals when you explore a woodland, because most mammals are active from dusk (sunset) to dawn (sunrise). Also, many mammals are shy of people.

Even though you can't see bobcats, rabbits and foxes, you can look for clues that they and other woodland animals have left behind.

You are a detective searching for clues left by animals. Can you find all these clues? Look carefully . . . describe what you find. Who do you think made the clues?

I Found It ✔   Who I Think Made the Clue:

○ Bird Nest _____

○ Burrow/Tunnel _____

○ Scat (animal droppings) _____

○ Fur _____

○ Feathers _____

○ Bones _____

○ Eggshells _____

○ Animal trails _____

○ Tracks _____

○ Partially eaten leaf _____

○ Shedded skin _____

○ Other evidence _____

ANIMAL TRACKS

Your foot is shaped differently than a mouse's foot. Each species of animal has its own tracks. You can use tracks to learn which animals live in an area. To identify the animal tracks you find, count the number of toes and study the shape of the track. Like this

2-toed tracks = **hoofed animals**
(deer, moose, elk)

4-toed tracks with **no** claw marks = **cat family**
(bobcats, mountain lions, house cats). Cats have <u>retractable</u> claws and walk with their claws tucked inside.

4-toed tracks **with** claw marks = **dog family**
(foxes, dogs, coyotes, wolves). Dogs do not have <u>retractable</u> claws so their claws are always "out."

FRONT

HIND
4-toed tracks with back foot larger than front foot = **rabbits, hares**

4-toed front feet and
5-toed back feet = **most rodents**
(shrews, mice, voles, squirrels)

5-toed front feet and
5-toed back feet = **opposums, raccoons**

FRONT

5-toed front feet and
5-toed back feet, foot like
= **bears**
...**and you!**

HIND

GONE TRACKIN'

On the next two pages draw animal tracks
you find. Some things to look for:
- shape of the tracks
- number of toes
- claw marks
- if you have a measuring tape, measure
  the length and width of the tracks. Is the
  front foot smaller than the back foot?

Example Track:

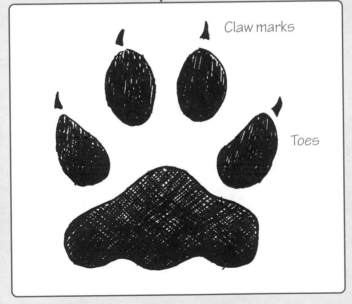

Claw marks

Toes

2½ inches

2½ inches

Dog or Coyote

You can use a track book to identify the
animals that made the tracks you found.

ANIMAL TRACKS I FOUND

*"Hmmm. I wonder who
these belong to?"*

44

ANIMAL TRACKS I FOUND

MY WOODLAND NOTES & SKETCHES

MY WOODLAND NOTES & SKETCHES

MY WOODLAND NOTES & SKETCHES

My Woodland Notes & Sketches

MEADOWS

IT'S A SMALL WORLD

A meadow is full of small things. A hopping grasshopper. A colorfu
flower. A patient spider sitting on its web. A fluffy seed floating
through the air. If you look closely at the small things, you will find
that a meadow is a busy place!

How many small things can you find in your meadow?

**Search the meadow for small things. Use a
magnifying glass if you have one. Try to find
things that are the size of the circles on the next
page. If you want, you can draw what you
find in each circle** (you may have to draw the
really small things outside the circles and make
them bigger than they really are).

WHY DO PLANTS HAVE FLOWERS?

Why do plants have flowers with bright colors, interesting shapes and sweet scents? To attract pollinators!

Insects, birds and bats are pollinators. They visit flowers to drink **nectar** and as they feed, grains of **pollen** rub onto their bodies. When they feed at another plant, the pollen rubs off their bodies onto the new flowers. This is **pollination**. Plants need to spread pollen to **reproduce**.

INSECTS: Most flowers are pollinated by insects. Many flowers smell sweet to attract insects which get much of their daily food from the nectar they find in the blooms.

BIRDS: Many bird-pollinated flowers are brightly colored, because birds have good color vision. However, many of these flowers have no scent, because most birds have a poor sense of smell.

BATS: Flowers pollinated by bats have large white petals, because bats are active at night. These flowers also have strong, unpleasant scents, because bats like musty, foul smells.

So now you know why plants have flowers . . . to attract pollinators!

 FLOWERS I FOUND

Flowers are wonderful to draw, because they are colorful and they don't run away! Explore the meadow for flowers . . . how many colors do you see? In the space below and on the next two pages you can draw the flowers you find.

FLOWERS I FOUND

Flowers I Found

TODAY'S DATE: _____ PLACE: _____

These are my wishes for the Earth .
I wish … _____

Ladybug

_____

_____

_____

_____

_____

_____

_____

_____

_____

_____

_____

_____

_____

_____

_____

_____

_____

_____

_____

_____

_____

_____

_____

_____

_____

Plants Can't Walk

Imagine you are a plant with seeds you want to **disperse** (travel to a new location) so they can grow in a new place. How are you going to move your seeds?

You can't walk, but you can make "containers" around your seeds to help them travel without you. This is what plants do. Plants use wind, water and animals (including people) to disperse their seeds.

Here's how they do it:

Helicopter method -- Seeds with **wings** are dispersed by the wind.

Parachute method -- Seeds with **fluffy hairs** are dispersed by the wind.

Rocket Ship method -- Some seeds have **exploding** containers. The seeds burst out of the container and fly through the air.

Eat and Run method -- Seeds inside **fruit** are dispersed by animals. An animal eats the fruit and swallows the seeds, which go through the animal's body and drop to the ground in scat (droppings).

Hitchhiker method -- Seeds with **spikes** or **barbs** are dispersed by animals and people. The seeds get caught in animals' fur or people's socks and travel to a new location as the animal or person walks away.

§EED §CAVENGER ♯UNT

Explore the meadow for seeds. Can you find every-thing listed on the two Seed Scavenger Hunt pages? If you have a magnifying glass, take a closer look at the seeds you find. Draw a sketch of each kind of seed you find. (The best time to find seeds is in summer and fall.)

I Found It ✔

◯ *Seeds with **wings**. (Toss a seed into the air -- watch it fly)*

My drawing:

◯ *Seeds with **fluffy hairs**. (Blow on a seed and follow it. See how far it travels before it lands)*

My drawing:

ꙅEED ꙅCAVENGER ꙌUNT

I Found It ✔

◯ *Seeds with **spikes or barbs**. (Check your socks!)*

My drawing:

◯ *Seeds that **animals might eat**. (Don't eat them yourself!)*

My drawing:

The **smallest** seed I found was this size:	The **largest** seed I found was this size:
*My drawing of my **favorite** seed*	*My drawing of the **funniest looking** seed*

"Ha Ha"

My Nature Writings: Ways I Can Help Nature

These are ways I can help nature.
I can help nature by . . . _____

_____

_____

_____

_____

_____

_____

_____

_____

_____

_____

_____

_____

_____

_____

_____

_____

_____

_____

_____

_____

_____

_____

_____

WHAT IS AN INSECT?

Did you know that more than half of the world's living creatures are insects? And scientists believe there are millions of insects we haven't even discovered yet!

So, what is an insect? All insects, from beetles to butterflies, have the same basic body structure:

• A **BODY** in **3** parts . . .

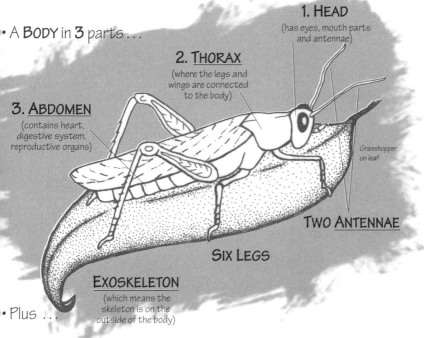

1. HEAD
(has eyes, mouth parts and antennae)

2. THORAX
(where the legs and wings are connected to the body)

3. ABDOMEN
(contains heart, digestive system, reproductive organs)

Grasshopper on leaf

TWO ANTENNAE

SIX LEGS

EXOSKELETON
(which means the skeleton is on the outside of the body)

• Plus . . .

. . . and most insects have
TWO PAIRS OF WINGS
(some have no wings)

 MY INSECT

Create your own insect. Make sure you have all the parts of an insect in your drawing.

IF I WERE AN INSECT...

...I WOULD LOOK LIKE THIS

Explore the meadow for insects. If you have a magnifying glass, examine an insect closely. How do you know it is an insect? (Look back on page 63).

On the next page, draw or write about the insects you found.

Word of CAUTION: Some insects bite or pinch. It is best not to touch or hold an insect unless you know it will not hurt you. If you don't know, then don't touch!

•• **Thank You For Treating Insects With Respect** ••

INSECTS I FOUND

BUTTERFLY OR MOTH?

Do you know how to tell butterflies from moths? Here's how...

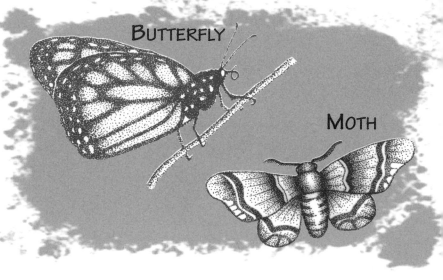

BUTTERFLY

MOTH

MOST BUTTERFLIES...

have **bright** colors
fly in **daytime**
rest with **wings together**
have **straight** antennae with knobs

MOST MOTHS...

have **dull** colors
fly at **night**
rest with **wings apart**
have **feathery or straight** antennae
  without knobs

**On the next page, draw the butterflies
and moths you see.**

*Maybe butterflies should be called "flutter bys"...
because that's what they do.
They flutter by!*

MY BUTTERFLIES

MY MOTHS

SPIDERS ARE SPINNERS!

Insects cannot spin webs, but spiders can! Spiders are different from insects in many ways.

Spiders have . . .

8 EYES
(most have 8; some
have 6, 4 or 2 eyes)

**BODY IN
2 PARTS**
1. **Cephalothorax**
(head and thorax
combined)
2. Abdomen

**SENSORY
HAIRS**
(for a good sense
of touch)

8 LEGS

SPIDERS MAKE SILK
(for travelling, wrapping food,
making webs & egg cases)

Spiders might look a bit scary, but they are very important. If there were no spiders, the world's insect population would grow out of control, because insects are spiders' favorite food.

Look at how big you are compared to a spider. Imagine how scared a spider might feel about **you!**

Explore the meadow for spiders. Have fun filling out the spider pages.

MY SPIDER PAGE

Spider webs come in different shapes. How many different shapes can you find?

Draw your favorite spider webs here . . .

My Spider Page

Find a small meadow you can explore. Guess how many spider webs there are in the meadow.

I guess there are_____ spider webs.

Now count all the spider webs you can find.

I found _____ spider webs.

Was your guess close to what you found?

The **smallest** *spider I found was this size* (draw a circle the size of the spider's body . . . and show how long its legs were)

_____

The **largest** *spider I found was this size* (draw a circle the size of the spider's body . . .and show how long its legs were)

Word of CAUTION: Some spiders do bite, so look but don't touch.

MY SPIDER PAGE

Look closely at a spider you find (use a magnifying glass if you have one). **Draw a picture of the spider.**

How many legs does it have? Is it hairy? Can you see its eyes?

My Spider

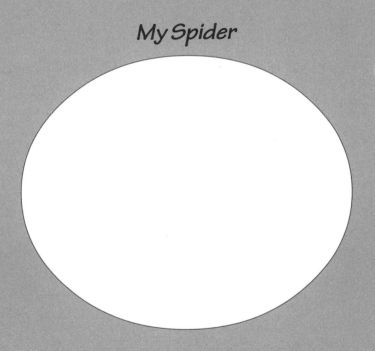

•• **Thank You For Treating Spiders With Respect** ••

If I Were a Reptile

If you were a reptile, you would . . .

- Have tough scales to protect your body.
- Be cold-blooded. The temperature of your body depends on the temperature of the environment. (This is why reptiles bask in the sun, especially in the morning).
- Lay eggs with tough leathery shells on land.
- Have a skeleton, including a backbone.

But you are not a reptile. Who is? Snakes, lizards and turtles are. And a sunny meadow can be a good place to find snakes and lizards (turtles are usually near water).

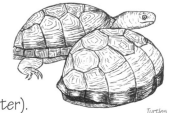

Turtles

Explore the meadow for reptiles. Keep a list of reptiles you find in the Nature List at the back of your journal. You can also use the blank pages at the end of this section for your reptile sketches.

Lizard

Word of CAUTION: It can be harmful to you and to the reptiles to catch and hold them. In this activity, use your eyes and not your hands.

MAGICAL MEADOW

Buzzing bees. Bright flowers. Floating seeds.
Sweet grasses. All these make meadows feel
magical.

Find your favorite place in the meadow. Look
around you . . . what do you see? Close your
eyes and listen . . . what do you hear? Feel the
ground under you and the air against your skin.
How does it feel?

What are your thoughts as you sit in the meadow?
How do you feel being here?

On the next two pages, draw and write about
your magical meadow.

MY FAVORITE MEADOW PLACE

My favorite place is located _____

_____

I see _____

_____

_____

_____

I hear _____

_____

_____

_____

I feel _____

_____

_____

_____

I think _____

_____

_____

_____

MY DRAWING OF MY FAVORITE PLACE

MY MEADOW NOTES & SKETCHES

MY MEADOW NOTES & SKETCHES

MY MEADOW NOTES & SKETCHES

MY MEADOW NOTES & SKETCHES

MY MEADOW NOTES & SKETCHES

MY MEADOW NOTES & SKETCHES

PONDS and STREAMS

TODAY'S DATE: _____ PLACE: _____

THE WORLD . . .

Here you are, by a pond or stream. Before you go any further, take some time to write in these two journal pages and get to know the world by the water.

FIRST IMPRESSION - *The first thing I noticed at this pond or stream was . . .* _____

_____
_____
_____
_____

DESCRIPTION - *This is my description of this pond or stream:*

_____
_____
_____
_____
_____

SOUNDS ALL AROUND - *These are the sounds I hear:*

_____
_____
_____
_____

... BY THE WATER

PLANTS GROWING - These are the kinds of plants I see growing: _____

_____
_____
_____
_____
_____

ANIMAL ACTIVITY - These are the animals or evidence of animals (tracks, homes, feathers) I see: _____

_____
_____
_____
_____

LAST IMPRESSION - This is what I want to remember about this pond or stream: _____

_____
_____
_____
_____
_____

AMPHIBIANS -- ANIMALS OF LAND & WATER

The word **amphibian** means "double-life." Frogs, salamanders and newts are called amphibians, because they live a double life in water and on land. They live in water while they are young and they live on land as adults.

Amphibians have moist skin and most live in cool, damp places where they won't dry out. Most amphibians lay their eggs in water. Amphibians, like reptiles, are cold-blooded.

SEARCH FOR SALAMANDERS

Gently lift rocks and logs . . . do you see salamanders? If you do, look but don't touch; salamanders have sensitive skin.

When you are finished looking, slowly set the rock or log back in place being careful not to smash the salamander.

FROGS

The most commonly seen amphibians are frogs.

Frogs live everywhere, even in cold places.
They survive the cold by
hibernating which is a long sleep when
they do not move or eat.

Frogs are most noticeable in spring when we
can hear and see them. Male frogs sing
to attract females.
The females are usually silent.

When a male and female meet, the
female lays her eggs
in the water and
the male **fertilizes**
the eggs. After the eggs are fertilized,
most frogs abandon
their eggs.

Spring and summer are good
times to explore the water
for frog eggs and tadpoles.

**Draw a picture of
a frog you see . . .**

**or maybe a frog
you'd like to see!**

"Ribbit"

Frog Life Cycle

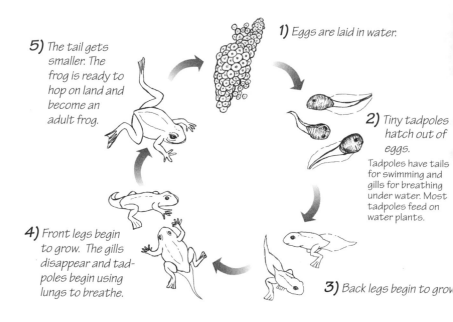

5) The tail gets smaller. The frog is ready to hop on land and become an adult frog.

1) Eggs are laid in water.

2) Tiny tadpoles hatch out of eggs.

Tadpoles have tails for swimming and gills for breathing under water. Most tadpoles feed on water plants.

4) Front legs begin to grow. The gills disappear and tadpoles begin using lungs to breathe.

3) Back legs begin to grow.

CALLING ALL FROGS AND FUTURE FROGS

Explore the water for frog eggs and tadpoles. You will probably find eggs during spring and tadpoles during summer.

If you have a large container, you can gently scoop up a tadpole to see it more closely (make sure it's in water). Does it have legs yet? Is the tadpole breathing through gills or lungs?

Can you find frogs? Record what you find on the next page.

I FOUND 'EM

I found FROG EGGS!   *They look like this . . .*

. . . and this is how many I saw: _____

I found TADPOLES!   *They look like this . . .*

. . . and this is how many I saw: _____

I found FROGS!   *They look like this . . .*

. . . and this is how many I saw: _____

**Be sure you leave all eggs, tadpoles and
frogs where you found them. Thank you!**

INSECTS IN WATER

It's great fun to search for **aquatic** insects in ponds, streams and
rivers. You would be amazed at how many aquatic insects there are
About 5,000 species of insects in North America spend all or part
of their lives in water! Some insects -- like water beetles -- live in
water their entire lives. Other insects, such as dragonfly **nymphs**,
only spend the first part of their lives in water.

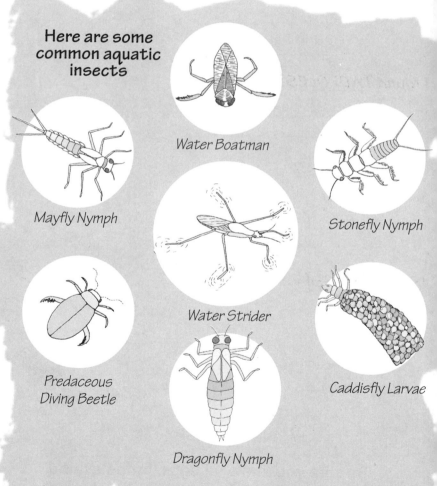

**Here are some
common aquatic
insects**

Water Boatman

Mayfly Nymph

Stonefly Nymph

Water Strider

Predaceous
Diving Beetle

Dragonfly Nymph

Caddisfly Larvae

Stream Study

You can find insects in or at the surface of the water and on rocks at the bottom of shallow water. It's a good idea to have these tools to help you explore for aquatic insects:

- dip net
- small container filled with water
- magnifying box or magnifying glass
- a paint brush (use to gently brush insects from rocks into container)
- an aquatic insect identification book.

PLEASE FOLLOW THESE RULES: Remember that aquatic insects must always be in water. Put only one insect in your container at a time and please be sure to put insects back where you found them. Always be with another person when you are exploring near water. Have fun!

On the next two pages, draw the aquatic insects you find. Write notes about each insect, such as . . .
- **name of insect (if you know it)**
- **where you found it**
- **what it was doing**
- **anything special you notice**

•• Thank You For Being Gentle With Aquatic Insects ••

I FOUND AQUATIC INSECTS

Insect I found: _____

Where I found it: _____

What it was doing: _____

Something I noticed: _____

_____

Insect I found: _____

Where I found it: _____

What it was doing: _____

Something I noticed: _____

_____

Insect I found: _____

Where I found it: _____

What it was doing: _____

Something I noticed: _____

_____

I Found Aquatic Insects

Insect I found: _____

Where I found it: _____

What it was doing: _____

Something I noticed: _____

_____

Insect I found: _____

Where I found it: _____

What it was doing: _____

Something I noticed: _____

_____

Insect I found: _____

Where I found it: _____

What it was doing: _____

Something I noticed: _____

_____

TODAY'S DATE: _____ PLACE: _____

Jackrabbit

My Nature Writings: Why I Like Being in Nature

I like being in nature because . . .

_____

_____

_____

_____

_____

_____

_____

_____

_____

_____

_____

_____

_____

_____

_____

_____

_____

_____

_____

_____

_____

_____

_____

_____

_____

_____

_____

_____

ADAPTATIONS

Aquatic insects have special __adaptations__ to help them live in water. An adaptation is a physical characteristic or a behavior that helps an animal survive in its environment.

All aquatic insects have adaptations to help them *eat, breathe, move* and *protect* themselves.

Aquatic Insect	Adaptation . . .
Dragonfly nymph	. . . *to eat,* the dragonfly nymph has a sharp flap at its mouth that shoots out and spears prey.
Water beetle	. . . *to breathe,* the water beetle traps air on hairs under its body or under its wing cases. When the beetle dives under water, it breathes from those bubbles.
Water strider	. . . *to move,* the water strider has oily hairs on its legs that enable it to walk on water.
Caddisfly larvae	. . . *to protect,* the caddisfly larvae builds a protective case around itself using pebbles, plants and sticks to hide from __predators__.

CREATURE FEATURE

Create your own aquatic creature. It can be anything, but make sure your creature has special adaptations to eat, breathe, move and protect itself in water. Draw a picture of your creature in the space below and write about your creature on the next page.

MY CREATURE FEATURE

MY CREATURE FEATURE

My creature's name is: _____

How it eats: _____

_____

_____

_____

_____

_____

How it breathes: _____

_____

_____

_____

_____

How it moves: _____

_____

_____

_____

_____

How it protects itself: _____

_____

_____

_____

_____

Birds

Have you ever imagined yourself flying . . . soaring high in the sky?
You see the world beneath you -- tree tops, city streets, a river
flowing through a valley. You feel the wind blowing
on your face. Flying is wonderful!

Why can birds fly, when we can't?

Hawk

LIGHT AS A FEATHER

Birds are built to fly. Two **adaptations** that help birds fly are . . .

1. LIGHTWEIGHT SKELETON

Birds have a minimum number of bones and many bird bones are hollow, so a bird's skeleton usually weighs less than its feathers. Birds have lightweight beaks instead of teeth which are heavy. They have fewer joints than people have which means fewer heavy muscles.

2. FEATHERS

Feathers are lightweight, strong and flexible. They help birds to fly and stay warm. Birds have different kinds of feathers:

shaft

down

DOWN FEATHERS	SEMIPLUME FEATHERS	CONTOUR FEATHERS
(small, fluffy feathers located next to skin -- help **insulate** birds)	(have a shaft and down -- are under the contour feathers, fill out the body and **insulate**)	(with stiff shaft, form outline of bird's body -- outer body feathers, wings and tail)

Birds replace all their feathers each year, some two or three times a year.

Search for feathers. Can you tell if a feather is a down, semiplume or contour feather?

(You will find the most feathers during spring and summer. Why do you think this is?)

Birds I Have Seen

Use these two pages to draw pictures of birds you see. If you want, you can try to identify each bird using a field guide that has pictures of birds.

I Saw These, Too

BIRDWATCHING...

This is a birdwatching activity. You don't need to know the names of the birds you see. Just look closely at the birds and what they are doing.

Read the chart. If you find a bird that matches one of the squares, put an "X" through that square. Can you cross out all the squares?

A bird **flapping its wings** as it flies	A bird **soaring** high in the air
A bird **hopping**	A **flock** of birds flying
A bird **feeding** in the air	A bird with **webbed feet**
A bird **bathing**	A bird **in a tree**
A bird with a **sharp beak**	A bird **feeding underwater**
A bird with **yellow**	A bird with **stripes**

... BINGO

Birdwatching hints:
- Be quiet,
- Move slowly, and
- Listen carefully.
- If you have binoculars, look for birds
  with your eyes and when you see one,
  raise your binoculars to your eyes.

Songbird

A bird **diving**	A bird **singing**
A bird **hovering**	A bird **walking**
A bird with a **curved beak**	A bird with **sharp talons**
A bird with **blue**	A bird with a **long beak**
A bird **feeding on the ground**	A bird with **dots**
A bird **making a nest**	A bird all **one color**

TODAY'S DATE: _____ PLACE: _____

My Nature Writings: Why Nature is Special to Me

Nature is special to me because . . .

_____

_____

_____

_____

_____

_____

_____

_____

_____

_____

_____

_____

_____

_____

_____

_____

_____

_____

_____

_____

_____

_____

_____

_____

_____

_____

Egret

TODAY'S DATE: _____ PLACE: _____

My Nature Writings: Why I Think Nature is Important

I think nature is important because . . .

_____
_____
_____
_____
_____
_____
_____
_____
_____
_____
_____
_____
_____
_____
_____
_____
_____
_____
_____
_____
_____
_____
_____
_____
_____
_____
_____
_____

Simple Words Create...

Everyone, including you, can write poetry. Poems don't have to rhyme. They don't have to be long. Poems can be very simple. Here are some forms of poetry that are simple and beautiful.

HAIKU
(pronounced "hi-coo")

A haiku poem has 3 lines:

Line 1 = 5 syllables
Line 2 = 7 syllables
Line 3 = 5 syllables

Example

**darting dragonflies
fly over rushing water
fish watching below**

CINQUAIN
(pronounced "sin-kwane")

A cinquain has 5 lines:

Line 1 = 1 word: title
Line 2 = 2 words: describe title
Line 3 = 3 words: describe action
Line 4 = 4 words: describe feeling
Line 5 = 1 word: similar to title word

Example

**river
green blue
rushing singing falling
happy soothed quiet excited
water**

FREE VERSE

In a free verse poem, you write your poem any way you like.

Example

**Sitting by this stream,
I am as smooth as the
rocks, as fresh as
the air, as free
as the water.**

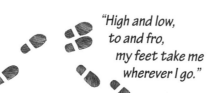

*"High and low,
to and fro,
my feet take me
wherever I go."*

... BEAUTIFUL POETRY

Now it's your turn.

Find a comfortable place to sit at a pond, lake, stream or river. Sit quietly for a few moments. Close your eyes. What words come to you?

On the next two pages of your journal, write poems about where you are.

Choose any form of poetry you like. You can also draw pictures next to your poems.

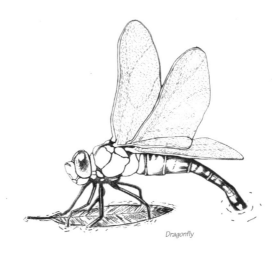

Dragonfly

MY POEMS

 MY POEMS

My Pond & Stream Notes & Sketche

My Pond & Stream Notes & Sketches

MY POND & STREAM NOTES & SKETCHES

My Pond & Stream Notes & Sketches

SEASHORE

Seashore Treasures

Treasures aren't only found in a

There are treasures to be found on a SANDY BEACH! You probably won't find gold coins or rubies, but you can find other treasures jus as beautiful.

Where can you find seashore treasures? Try searching the high tid mark. Twice a day, the ocean rises up the shore and then retreats. The high tide mark is where the ocean rises the farthest and it is here that the waves deposit all sorts of sea treasures.

What might you find at the high tide mark?

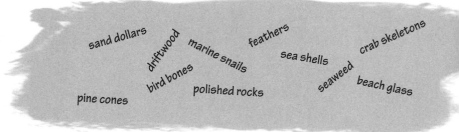

sand dollars
driftwood
bird bones
pine cones
marine snails
polished rocks
feathers
sea shells
seaweed
crab skeletons
beach glass

You might also find living treasures, such as a seal pup or a flock of seabirds. But remember not to disturb or approach wild animals.

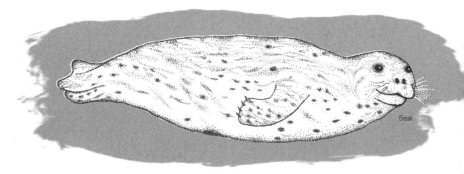

Seal

BE A PIRATE!

Aye matie . . . be a pirate and search for seashore treasure! Explore the seashore high and low -- examine seaweed, turn over rocks (remember to return them), and dig in the sand. What hidden treasures wait to be discovered?

When you find a treasure . . . a seashell more beautiful than a diamond or a crab's claw more valuable than gold . . . instead of putting it in your pocket, write about or draw it in your TREASURE TROVE list. This list describes all the seashore treasures you discover in your pirate adventures.

Sea Coral

Should you take your treasures home? It's better to leave your treasures on the beach so other "pirates" can discover them too.

Sand Dollar

If every person took treasures home, there would be nothing left.

But some things don't belong on the seashore -- cans, plastics, bottles and other litter -- these are all good things to take away from the seashore.

Sea Shell

MY SEASHORE TREASURE TROVE

These are the amazing treasures I found at the seashore . .

My Seashore Treasure Trove

MY MESSAGE IN A BOTTLE

Imagine writing a message, putting it in a bottle and throwing it into the ocean. At first it bobs up and down in the surf until a current carries it out to sea. Your bottle floats in the ocean for a long time and has many adventures. A bird lands on it. A pod of dolphins plays with it. After many months at sea your bottle finally washes up onto a seashore on the other side of the world.

One morning, a child in a far away country finds your bottle half-buried in the sand. The child picks up your bottle, notices the paper inside and pulls out your message. It says . . .

- What would you want your message to say?
- What would you write about yourself and where you live?
- What would you want that child on the other side of the world to know about you?

Write your message on the next page in your journal.

A MESSAGE ABOUT ME

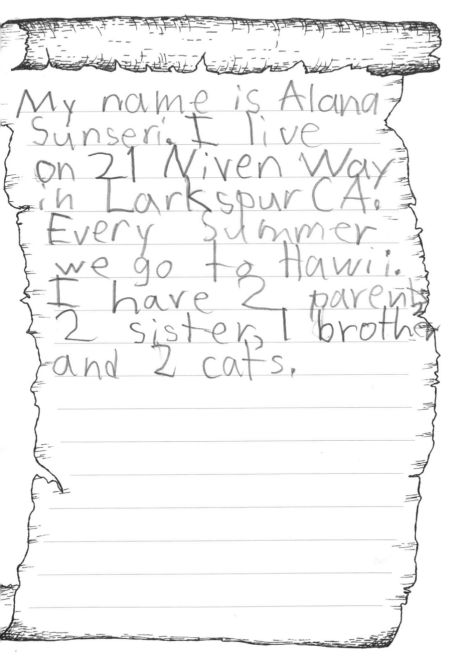

My name is Alana
Sunseri. I live
on 21 Niven Way
in Larkspur CA.
Every Summer
we go to Hawii.
I have 2 parents
2 sisters, 1 brother
and 2 cats.

PLANET TIDEPOOL

You don't have to go to another planet to see strange creatures . . . just visit a tidepool.

What is a tidepool? Tidepools are located on rocky shores. During high tide, the rocks are covered by water. But when the tide is low, the rocks are exposed and pools of water are left behind in the rocks. The best time to explore tidepools is at low tide.

You will find different creatures in different parts of the tidepools.

On high rocks are animals that can be **out of the water**, such as mussels.

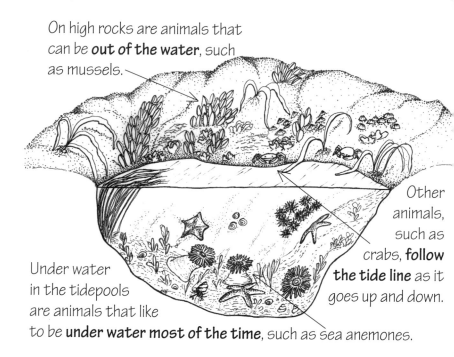

Other animals, such as crabs, **follow the tide line** as it goes up and down.

Under water in the tidepools are animals that like to be **under water most of the time**, such as sea anemones.

On the rocks and in the pools you will find bizarre creatures that will fill you with wonder!

GET A GRIP!

Living on a rocky shore is not an easy life. Waves crash down, the tide comes in and goes out, the wind blows hard and the sun is hot. In order to survive on the rocky shores, all tidepool creatures must have a way to anchor themselves onto rocks . . .

ADULT BARNACLES live inside volcano-shaped cases permanently stuck to rocks with a special cement.

MUSSELS attach themselves to rocks by releasing a liquid that turns hard in seawater.

SEA STARS have hundreds of tube feet with suction cups that help them to hold on tight.

SEA URCHINS grip the rocks using tube feet with suction cups. The tube feet are in-between the spikes.

ANEMONES attach to rocks, but can move around (slowly!). Anemone tentacles have stinging cells. You can touch the tentacles, but be gentle.

CRABS have flat bodies that allow them to wedge themselves into crevices in the rocks.

Can you find these tidepool creatures? Use the next two pages to draw pictures of the creatures you find in tidepools.

TIDEPOOL CREATURES I FOUND

Be a Good Explorer and Be Safe!
- Always walk -- don't run. Tidepools are slippery places.
- Always face the ocean and look out for waves.
- Keep tidepool creatures in their tidepools. Never move an animal to a different tidepool.
- Don't pull animals off rocks. If you have to use force to pick up an animal, don't pick it up. If you do, you can rip their "feet" off. *Ouch!*
- Watch where you walk. Be careful not to step on animals.

•• Thank You For Being Careful When You Explore Tidepools ••

I Found These, Too!

"Awesome"

Rocks to Pebbles to Sand

If you are standing on a pebble beach right now, the pebbles under your feet will someday be sand! Pebbles get a tiny bit smaller with each wave that washes over them.

Over hundreds of years the ocean grinds rocks into pebbles . . .

. . . and pebbles into sand.

A pebble beach is a difficult place for animals and plants to live. The motion of the waves smashes pebbles together so that animals and plants attached to the pebbles get crushed. You won't find many creatures or plants living on pebbles . . .

. . . but a pebble beach is a great place to find pebbles! Pebbles come in many sizes, shapes and colors. They can be beautiful, especially when they are wet.

How many pebbles can you find that match the Pebble Chart? If you find a pebble that matches the chart, draw a picture of the pebble in the square.

Word of CAUTION: While you're doing this activity, always face the ocean and keep an eye out for waves. Search for pebbles on the beach, not in the water.

MY PEBBLE CHART

A pebble with **stripes**	A pebble with **green**	A pebble with **dots**
A **black and white** pebble	A piece of **shell**	A **flat** pebble
A **round** pebble	My **favorite** pebble	A **polished** pebble
A **multi-colored** pebble	A **bumpy** pebble	A pebble with **blue**
A pebble all **one color**	The **strangest** pebble I see	A piece of **smooth glass**

SEA MONSTER

For hundreds of years sailors have claimed that sea monsters dwell in the depths of the ocean. Folk tales from all over the world tell of fantastic ocean creatures:

- In Viking legends, ocean storms were said to be caused by the movements of a giant sea serpent.

- Norwegian folklore tells about a giant sea monster called a kraken that attacked ships with its long tentacles (maybe the really encountered a giant squid!).

- Stories of mermaids -- creatures that are half woman and half fish -- have been told for 3,000 years. It was said that mermaids lured sailors into danger with their songs.

If you could make up an imaginary "sea monster", what would you create? Keep in mind that your ocean creature doesn't have to be dangerous . . . it can be anything you want it to be.

Draw a picture of your ocean creature and write a story about it.

MY SEA MONSTER

MY SEASHORE NOTES & SKETCHES

My Seashore Notes & Sketches

My Seashore Notes & Sketches

My Seashore Notes & Sketches

TWILIGHT

MAGICAL TWILIGHT

The setting sun brings the day to an end. Soon the sky will darken and stars will shine. Twilight is the time between day and night -- after the sun has set and before the sky is dark.

Twilight is a wonderful time to be outside. You can watch the setting of the sun, the changing colors of the sky and spot the first star to shine.

SUNSET SIT

Find a comfortable place outside where you can watch the sun set. Begin your sunset sit before the sun has "touched" the horizon.

Watch the colors of the sky change. Listen to the sounds around you. Feel the air on your skin.

As you watch the sun setting below the horizon, write words that describe what you see, hear and feel. Write words that describe the setting of the sun and the beginning of twilight.

You can also draw a sketch of the sunset to go along with your words.

How long does it take for the sun to set -- from when it "touches" the horizon until it just disappears?

A SUNSET IS TO ME...

COMMON SENSE

Imagine you are a **nocturnal** (night-active) animal. In the darkness of night, how do you find food to eat? How do you avoid **predators**? How do you move around without getting lost?

You use your senses: sight, hearing, smell, taste and touch. Nocturnal animals use one or more of their senses to help them survive in darkness.

SIGHT:

Bobcats have large light-sensitive eyes that help them see in low light.

HEARING:

Great Horned Owls use their highly sensitive hearing to hunt mice or other prey on the ground.

SMELLS:

Moles live underground where it is always dark and find their food -- worms -- using their sense of smell.

TOUCH:

Mice use their long whiskers to feel their surroundings without making any sound.

Twilight is a great time to observe animals because the day-active (**diurnal**) animals are heading to their rest places for the night, while the night-active (nocturnal) animals are becoming active and leaving their "homes."

WHOOO COMES AROUND?

Spotted Owl

You can use your senses to observe animals during twilight. First, find a place where animals are active. (The edge of a meadow or near a stream are good places.) **Choose a place to sit where you blend in with the surroundings. Sit comfortably and quietly.**

Look all around you: in the sky, on the ground, in front of you and to each side. Listen for sounds. Were they made by an animal? Be watchful. On the next page, keep a list of the animals you hear and see.

GLOWING EYES: You can also use a flashlight to search for glowing eyes. Some nocturnal animals have a silvery membrane (called a **tapetum**) in the back of their eyes that reflects light so that their eyes glow or shine when they look into light.

Sometimes the color of the eye-shine can tell you what animal you are seeing:

Color	Animal
White	Deer
Bright White	Dog family (coyote, fox)
Yellowish	Cat family (bobcat, house cat)
Yellow	Raccoon
Dull Orange	Opossom
Bright Orange	Bear
Amber	Skunk

REMEMBER to be safe and always make sure an adult knows where you are.

MY LIST OF TWILIGHT ANIMALS

Animal   Date and Location

Badger

_____   _____

_____   _____

_____   _____

_____   _____

_____   _____

_____   _____

_____   _____

_____   _____

_____   _____

_____   _____

_____   _____

_____   _____

_____   _____

_____   _____

_____   _____

_____   _____

_____   _____

_____   _____

ECHOLOCATION

A mouse-eared bat can eat over 500 mosquitoes an hour! But how does a bat find mosquitoes in the dark? By using sound.

An insect-eating bat hunts by making high-pitched squeaks as it flies. When the squeak hits an object, the sound bounces back. The bat hears the echo and knows something is in the air. This is **echolocation.** (People usually cannot hear bat squeaks, because they are too high-pitched for our ears.)

Bats use echolocation to find mosquitoes and other flying insects in the dark.

Bat

Twilight is a great time to watch bats hunt. It is easiest to watch bats in a clear area, such as a meadow or by a pond. Write about bats on the next two pages of your journal.

BAT WRITING

I have seen bats
at these **Locations**...

...and this is
What They Were Doing

_____   _____

_____   _____

_____   _____

_____   _____

_____   _____

_____   _____

_____   _____

_____   _____

_____   _____

_____   _____

Here are some words or phrases I would use to **Describe Bats:**

_____

_____

_____

_____

BAT WRITING

This is *How I Feel About Bats...*

_____

_____

_____

_____

_____

BAT FACTS

Myth: *Bats fly in your hair and attack you.*

Truth: The only time bats might swoop near people's heads is when they are hunting for flying insects.

Myth: *Most bats have rabies*

Truth: Bats contract rabies no more frequently than any other animal.

Myth: *Bats are dangerous.*

Truth: Bats are not dangerous -- although like all wild animals, they should not be captured or handled. In fact, bats are helpful! Worldwide, they help control the insect population. Bats are also very important to rain forests because they help **pollinate** flowers and **disperse** seeds.

Myth: *All bats drink blood.*

Truth: Only three species of bats drink blood and these species are all found in South America. Most bats (70%) eat insects and others feed only on fruit and **nectar**.

DID YOU KNOW ...

• *There are almost 1,000 species of bats*

• *Bats are not blind*

• *Some bats live as long as 30 years*

• *Bats are the only mammals which fly.*

ORIGIN STORY

An origin story tells how something came to be. This is a story about how stars came to be:

Long ago, there were no stars. The night sky was completely black. This was before Hummingbird drank the nectar of 1,000 flowers. One spring, there were more flowers than anyone had ever seen. Hummingbird was so excited, she drank nectar from one flower, then another flower, then another, and another, and then still another. She drank so much nectar her belly was as big as your fist!

Hummingbird had so much energy from drinking the nectar that she flew non-stop all day and into the night. She flew high into the night sky -- higher than she had ever been.

Up, up, up! She flew until she reached the end of the night sky and her long, thin beak poked right through the night sky.

She started poking holes in the night sky everywhere. All through the night she poked, poked, poked.

Finally, she became tired and floated down to earth to rest. The next night all the animals, birds, fish, people, frogs and snakes looked up at the sky in wonder. They saw thousands of little lights twinkling. They named all those lights after the hummingbird who made them. Her name was Star.

It is simple to make up an origin story. Choose something about the night and create a story of how it came to be. For example ...

Why does Raccoon have a mask?
Why does the Sun change color when it sets?
How did Mouse get long whiskers?

Now it's your turn to write an origin story about the night on the next page.

TODAY'S DATE: _____ PLACE: _____

MY NIGHT ORIGIN STORY

_____

_____

_____

_____

_____

_____

_____

_____

_____

_____

_____

_____

_____

_____

_____

_____

_____

_____

_____

_____

_____

_____

_____

_____

_____

_____

_____

TODAY'S DATE: _____ PLACE: _____

My Nature Writings: Spending Time Alone in Nature

When I am alone in nature
I think about ... _____

_____

_____

_____

_____

_____

_____

_____

_____

_____

_____

_____

_____

_____

_____

_____

_____

_____

_____

_____

_____

_____

_____

_____

_____

_____

_____

Day Shift and Night Shift

Most insects, birds and animals are active in "shifts" -- the day shift or night shift. For example, a hawk hunts over a meadow during the day, but an owl hunts over the meadow at night. The hawk works the day shift and the owl works the night shift.

You can witness the day and night shifts in nature by visiting the same spot in the morning and in the evening.

Find a place in nature that has animal activity. It needs to be a place you can visit in the morning and in the evening.

Visit your place during the morning. Sit quietly and watch for activity. Listen for birds. Do you see them flying? Can you describe them? Can you find insects? What are they doing? Are flowers open or closed? Do you see any mammals?

Write or draw all your observations in the "My Place After Sunrise" section on the next page.

Next, visit your place after sunset. Sit quietly in your spot. Write or draw all your observations in the "My Place After Sunset" section.

Compare your place during the morning and in the evening. Do you notice any differences? What things are the same?

You can visit your place many times -- or try this activity in different locations.

MY PLACE AFTER SUNRISE

MY PLACE AFTER SUNSET

MOONLIGHT IS SUNLIGHT

Did you know that the moon has no light? Moonlight is actually the sun's light shining on the moon. So, moonlight is sunlight!

Sometimes we see only a part of the moon shining. Other times we see the whole moon shining. Why is this?

The moon moves through different phases. The phase of the moon at any time depends on the positions of the moon, the earth and the sun. The moon **orbits** around the earth and it takes 29 ½ days to go around. The sun stays still. Look at the picture to understand the phases of the moon.

Day 7
Half Moon

Only part of the light side is facing earth, so we see one-half of the moon.

Day 14
Full Moon

The lighted side of the moon is facing earth, so we see a full moon.

Day 1
New Moon

The lighted side of the moon is facing away from earth, so we cannot see the moon.

We again see just one-half of the moon.

Day 21
Half Moon

Sometimes the earth gets directly between the moon and the sun, blocking the sun's light. This is called a lunar eclipse. And sometimes the moon blocks the sun's light from reaching the earth. This is called a solar eclipse.

WATCHING THE MOON

You can see for yourself how the moon's phases change. Start this activity when you can see the moon clearly (either at night or during the day). Once you have found the moon, write the date and the time on your moon chart on the next page. Next, draw the shape of the moon.

Fill out your chart every night (or day) for a month and watch how the moon's phases change.

SUN

PLACE: _____

MY MOON PHASE CHART

Date: _____ Time: _____	Date: _____ Time: _____	Date: _____ Time: _____
Date: _____ Time: _____	Date: _____ Time: _____	Date: _____ Time: _____
Date: _____ Time: _____	Date: _____ Time: _____	Date: _____ Time: _____
Date: _____ Time: _____	Date: _____ Time: _____	Date: _____ Time: _____
Date: _____ Time: _____	Date: _____ Time: _____	Date: _____ Time: _____

MY MOON PHASE CHART

Date: _____ Time: _____

Date: _____ Time: _____

Date: _____ Time: _____

Date: _____ Time: _____

Date: _____ Time: _____

Date: _____ Time: _____

Date: _____ Time: _____

Date: _____ Time: _____

Date: _____ Time: _____

Date: _____ Time: _____

Date: _____ Time: _____

Date: _____ Time: _____

Date: _____ Time: _____

Date: _____ Time: _____

Date: _____ Time: _____

CONSTELLATIONS

Do you like to find pictures in clouds? If so, you might also like looking for pictures in stars. People have been finding pictures in the stars, or **constellations**, for a long time.

Egyptians may have been the first people to make pictures out of stars, but many constellations we know today are named after Greek and Roman myths and legends. Many constellations have stories that explain the picture. Long ago, people used constellations to tell time and to find directions at night.

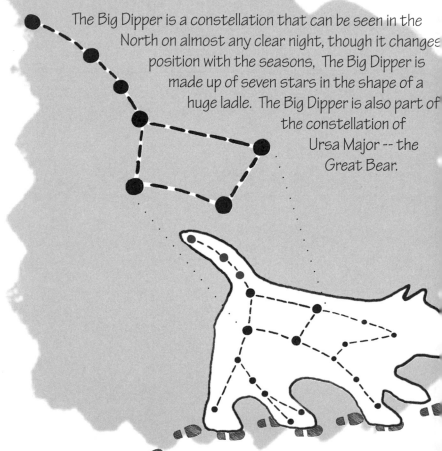

The Big Dipper is a constellation that can be seen in the North on almost any clear night, though it changes position with the seasons, The Big Dipper is made up of seven stars in the shape of a huge ladle. The Big Dipper is also part of the constellation of Ursa Major -- the Great Bear.

MAKE YOUR OWN CONSTELLATIONS

You can create your own constellations. On a clear night, look at the stars. Spend some time looking at all the different stars. Which are the brightest? Which are the faintest?

Look for shapes in the stars. Can you make any pictures?

Draw your star pictures below and on the next two pages of your journal. If you want, you can write a short story that explains your constellations in the sky.

MY CONSTELLATIONS

MY CONSTELLATIONS

MY TWILIGHT NOTES & SKETCHES

MY TWILIGHT NOTES & SKETCHES

My Twilight Notes & Sketches

MY TWILIGHT NOTES & SKETCHES

MY LAST PAGE

Have you finished My Nature Journal? If yes, you can write about your adventures, discoveries and feelings on this page.

These are my favorite activities and pages in My Nature Journal:

_____

_____

_____

_____

Something I learned while using My Nature Journal:

_____

_____

_____

_____

Something I always want to remember:

_____

_____

_____

_____

This is how I feel about nature after finishing My Nature Journal:

_____

_____

_____

_____

_____

**Always remember that your connection to nature
can last your whole life!**

MY NATURE LIST

This is my list of animals and plants
I have seen while exploring in nature.

MY NATURE LIST

MAMMALS

Animals	Where I Saw It / Notes

My Nature List

Birds

Birds   Where I Saw It / Notes

My Nature List

Amphibians

Amphibians	Where I Saw It / Notes
_____	_____
_____	_____
_____	_____
_____	_____
_____	_____
_____	_____
_____	_____
_____	_____
_____	_____

Reptiles

Reptiles	Where I Saw It / Notes
_____	_____
_____	_____
_____	_____
_____	_____
_____	_____
_____	_____
_____	_____
_____	_____

My Nature List

Insects

Insects	Where I Saw It / Notes

Fish

Fish	Where I Saw It / Notes

MY NATURE LIST

TREES

Trees

Where I Saw It / Notes

MY NATURE LIST

PLANTS and FLOWERS

Plants / Flowers   Where I Saw It / Notes

_____   _____

_____   _____

_____   _____

_____   _____

_____   _____

_____   _____

_____   _____

_____   _____

_____   _____

_____   _____

_____   _____

_____   _____

_____   _____

_____   _____

_____   _____

_____   _____

_____   _____

_____   _____

_____   _____

Glossary

abdomen - the last body section of an arthropod (insects, spiders, crustaceans).

adaptation - a physical characteristic or a behavior that helps an animal or plant survive in its environment.

amphibian - group of animals that are cold-blooded, have backbones, lay eggs and breathe through gills as juveniles and breathe air as adults.

antennae - the "feelers" located on an insect's head. Used to smell and taste.

aquatic - living in water.

broadleaf - the group of plants and trees having broad leaves that are not needles (as in evergreen trees).

carbon dioxide - the gas that is breathed out by animals and absorbed and used by plants in photosynthesis.

cephalothorax - the fused head and thorax of spiders and other arachnids, such as scorpions and ticks.

chlorophyll - the green chemical in plants that absorbs sunlight which is used in photosynthesis.

conifers - the group of trees that have seeds contained in cones.

constellations - any one of the 88 groups of stars, as determined by the International Astronomical Union.

deciduous - any tree that loses its leaves in winter, the end of the growing season.

decomposers - organisms, such as insects, bacteria and fungi, that feed on dead matter and break it into simpler substances, such as dirt.

disperse - to scatter, to be spaced widely.

diurnal - active during the day.

echolocation - locating an object by releasing sound and hearing the sound waves bounce off the object, creating an echo.

evergreen - plants and trees whose leaves remain green through more than one growing season.

excreted - to eliminate waste from the body.

exoskeleton - the outside, hard body covering of an insect or crustacean, such as a crab.

fertilize - to cause fertilization; when male and female sex cells join together to make one cell in order to produce offspring.

hibernating - to hibernate; to be inactive and restful during winter.

insulate - to cover with a material to prevent the transfer of heat.

invertebrate - an animal without a backbone.

nectar - a sugar liquid found in the flowers of plants and used to attract pollinators.

nocturnal - active during the night.

nymphs - an infant stage of life in some insects where the developing wings are present.

orbit - a circular path; to travel in circles.

oxygen - a gas in the air that is released by plants and breathed in by animals.

photosynthesis - the process by which green plants use the energy of sunlight to change carbon dioxide and water into sugars.

pigments - a coloring matter in plants and animals located in cells or tissue.

pollen - a powdery substance, produced by flowers, that contains male sex cells -- often yellow in color.

pollination - the transfer of pollen from the male part (stamen) of one flower to the female part (pistil) of another flower. This causes fertilization.

predator - an animal that hunts and kills another animal for food.

reproduce - how plants and animals produce offspring.

retractable - capable of being drawn in or drawn back.

sensory - relating to the senses (seeing, hearing, tasting, feeling and smelling).

species - a group of living things in which members of the group breed and produce offspring like themselves.

tapetum - a layer of tissue located in the eye that reflects light -- present in some species of animals.

thorax - the middle body section of an insect and other arthropods.

INDEX

WHAT I THINK ABOUT MY NATURE JOURNAL

Please tell us what you think about this book.

This is what I like about My Nature Journal

_____

_____

_____

_____

_____

This is what I would change or add to My Nature Journal

_____

_____

_____

_____

_____

Your name (optional)   _____

Your address (optional)   _____

                          _____

Your age (optional)   _____

After you write your comments, tear out this page (or make
a photocopy of it), place it in an envelope and mail to:

Adrienne Olmstead
Pa`jaro
3343 Las Huertas Rd.
Lafayette, CA 94549   THANK YOU!

TO ORDER ADDITIONAL COPIES

Please use this page (or make a photocopy) to order more copies of My Nature Journal.

Name _____

Address _____

City _____ State _____ Zip _____

	No. of Copies	Price	Total
My Nature Journal (1-10 copies)		$17^{95} ea.	
My Nature Journal (10 or more)		$14^{35} ea.	
(There is no charge for shipping)		Subtotal	
		California residents add 8.25% sales tax	
		TOTAL	

Payment by:

( ) check, payable to Pajaro

    credit card (check one):

    ( ) VISA ( ) MasterCard ( ) Discover ( ) American Express

Credit card no. __ __ __ __ __ __ __ __ __ __ __ __

Expiration date: (month) ____ year ____

Name printed on card _____

Signature (required) _____

MAIL order to:

Pa`jaro
3343 Las Huertas Rd.
Lafayette, CA 94549

or **FAX** credit card order to: **(925) 284 - 2642**

or **PHONE** (toll free): **1 - 877 - PAJARO 4**
(1- 877 - 725-2764)

or use our **WEB SITE**: **www.pajaro.com**

ABOUT THE AUTHOR

Tufted Puffin

Adrienne Olmstead developed a connection to nature at an early age. Her childhood summers were spent exploring meadows, forests and rivers. Her love of nature inspired her to attend the University of California, Santa Cruz where she received a degree in Environmental Studies.

Adrienne's career has been devoted to nature education. She has worked as a naturalist and as a director of environmental education programs. A creative and engaging educator, her respect for children and her appreciation of nature shine throughout her book.